𝕰x 𝕷ibris

Janusz R. P. Ostrowski

◈➤◦⬅◈

The Red Sea:

New and Selected Poems
1987 to 2011

Stephen Edgar

BASKERVILLE PUBLISHERS

Baskerville Publishers, Inc.
2455 Halloran Street
Fort Worth, Texas 76107
www.baskervillepublishers.com

Library of Congress Cataloging-in-Publication Data

Edgar, Stephen, 1951-
 The Red Sea : selected poems 1987 to 2011 / Stephen
 Edgar.
    p. cm.
ISBN 978-1-880909-78-2
I. Title.

PR9619.3.E23R43 2012
821'.914—dc23

                        2012010881

Manufactured in the United States of America

First Printing, 2012

To Clive James

Author's Note

I wish to thank the editors of the following, in which poems from "New Poems" have previously appeared: in the USA, in *Poetry*: "Auspices", "Murray Dreaming", "Lost to View", "Oswald Spengler Watches the Sunset", "Saccade", "The House of Time"; and in Australia, in *Meanjin*: "Inarticulate", "Precious Few", "Voyager"; in *HEAT*: "Lost World"; in *The Chimaera*: "The Annexe", "Time Out"; in *The Flea*: "Vertigo"; in *The Sun-Herald*: "Time Out".

The poems in "Selected Poems" are drawn from my following books, all published in Australia:
Corrupted Treasures (Melbourne: William Heinemann Australia, 1995): "Ulysses Burning", "The Secret Life of Books", "A Message from the Hills", "Chiaroscuro", "Reef".
Where the Trees Were (Canberra, Indigo/Ginninderra, 1999): "The Sail and the Gannet", "The Last Day", "Diversions of a Painter", "Penshurst", "The Menger Sponge".
Lost in the Foreground (Sydney, Duffy and Snellgrove, 2003): "The Complete Works", "Contents Page", "Incident at Grantley Manor", "Silk Screen", "The Shadow Maker", "Midas", "Sun Pictorial", "Elemental".
Other Summers (Melbourne, Black Pepper Publishing, 2006): "The Immortals", "Man on the Moon", "Eighth Heaven", "Living Colour", "Im Sommerwind", "Summer", "Diversionary Tactics".
History of the Day (Melbourne, Black Pepper Publishing, 2009): "Golden Coast", "Nocturnal", "Made to Measure", "The Red Sea", "Memorial", "The Grand Hotel", "Dreaming at the Speed of Light", "Coogee".

The last two books are available from Black Pepper Publishing at www.blackpepperpublishing.com .

"Oswald Spengler Watches the Sunset" is drawn from the opening paragraphs of the first chapter of Volume II of *The Decline of the West* by Oswald Spengler, translated by Charles Francis Atkinson.

Contents

New Poems

Lost to View

A range of clouds banked up behind the peak
Of that apocryphal
Blue mountain, with a wide, oblique
Burst of late sun
Projecting at the east's receding wall

A film of what the day so far has done:
A wind that tries to scrape
The breaking waves up as they run
Across the bay
And shatter at the foot of Fluted Cape

In tern and gannet-printed veils of spray;
And trees the wind has caught,
Which seem too self-contained to sway
When they are blown,
And only move as a pleasing afterthought.

No one. No human presence has been known,
Surely, to venture here.
It takes one blackbird to disown
That vagary
And, whistling just a few feet from his ear,

To call him back again and make him be
The subject in this scene,
The one who is required to see.
Another day,
No blackbird with its song will intervene.

The spray will hang its veils and the trees sway.

The Annexe

A small lit room,
With the undistinguished furnishings they love,
That Afghan rug of intricate design
You seem to be looking down on from above
At some great height—and, should the camera zoom,
The vistas, worlds, on hold
Within that pattern, line by woven line,
Would open and unfold.

The television,
With sound turned down, is flourishing its phantoms,
A synopticon in time-lapse of the ages
Where history can perform only in tantrums
Too quick to take in. Free of such misprision
A subdued music plays
Its tireless permutations and upstages
Time in more subtle ways

Philosophers
Would weep to hear. The windows are all blind
Now that the blinds are drawn, but on the walls
Their memories are suspended to remind
Whoever turns to look there what occurs,
Even without a viewer,
The moments that each pictured scene recalls
That somewhere may endure.

Two heads of hair
Above the sofa back they rest against
Are tilted to each other, where they grant
The omniscient narrator all that's sensed
Between them unobserved, all that they share,
To which the words they use,
These worn-out whispered nothings, are the scant
And ineffectual clues.

Outside the door,
Cold-lit and cold, the edifice is still,
Without a voice. The passages and stairs
Wind through the middle of the night until
Their pattern and the night are ever more
Inwoven, seen as though
From some great height, at which one scarcely dares
To gaze for vertigo.

Voyager

Out here where light becomes an apparition
Dispersed and flecked among the turning pattern
Of dusts and crystals and ice-crusted shards
That form the heaven-haunted rings of Saturn,
This frail scintilla brushes in its arc
Their powders and records them and discards
A wake of earthbound signals through the dark
That hides the passage of its boundless mission.

Fainter and fainter, ever more delayed,
The messages return out of the sky
To Earth. And Earth exhales to outer space
Its own intelligence, not in reply,
The mortal messages that are conveyed
Out of the world and leave no earthly trace.

Auspices

In siftings of chromatic sediment
Shed by the winter hours as they decay,
With slow descent
Light settles through the lower sky in peach,
Then mauve, then pale self-abnegating grey
Against the water, now that day is spent
At Bennetts Beach,

Under the high withdrawing blueness, band
On band, like layers in a decorative
Bottle of sand,
Enclosed beneath the heavens' dome, as though
This were the perfect realm in which to live,
Preserved, unburdened by the least demand,
Or wish, to know—

And simply be. Along the beach convene
Some silver gulls which stand around reflecting
Upon the sheen
That comes and goes about their scarlet feet,
And crested terns fly back and forth inspecting
The shallows for a last titbit to glean,
And lightly treat

A two-faced wind that works its way across
The metal of the sea it tries to planish
And to emboss,
While deep in its unbalanced buffetings
Gannets alternately appear and vanish,
Plunge, rise and loft and give their heads a toss.
These things, these things...

What future, though, in that simplicity?
If the observer alters what's observed,
Simple to see
The brilliant creatures may not long survive
Our scrutiny. And yet, what would be served
By aeons of extravagance to be
Merely alive,

Without the knowing eye, though its regard
Should bring to light what turns the world to stone?
Does the same hard
Attention that we boast of here abound,
Or has it been and gone among the starred
Immenseness—meaning we must fare alone,
Lost where we're found?

Beyond Yacaaba Head towards the east
The colours harboured in that sediment
Have been released
And all the lower sky is banked with ash,
Dulled to gunmetal grey. In the event
The gannets, calling it a day, have ceased
Their white panache.

Only the sandhills, looking west, declare
A citrine wash that seems to float adrift
Into the air,
Like some faint exhalation breathed upon
The night, in which a flock of ibis lift,
As though they had a mind to follow where
The light has gone.

Murray Dreaming

It's not the sharks
Sliding mere inches from his upturned face
Through warps of water where the tunnel arcs
Transparent overhead,
Their lipless jaws clamped shut, extruding teeth,
Their eyes that stare at nothing, like the dead,
Staring at him; it's not the eerie grace
Of rays he stood beneath,
Gaping at their entranced slow-motion chase

That is unending;
It's not the ultra-auditory hum
Of ET cuttlefish superintending
The iridescent craft
Of their lit selves, as messages were sent,
Turning the sight of him they photographed
To code: it is not this that left him dumb
With schoolboy wonderment
Those hours he wandered the aquarium.

It is that room,
That room of Murray River they had walled
In glass and, deep within the shifting gloom
And subtle drifts of sky
That filtered down, it seemed, from the real day
Of trees and bird light many fathoms high,
The giant Murray cod that was installed
In stillness to delay
All that would pass. The boy stood there enthralled.

Out in the day
Again, he saw the famous streets expound
Their theories about speed, the cars obey,
Racing to catch the sun,
The loud fast-forward crowds, and thought it odd
That in the multitudes not everyone
Should understand as he did the profound
Profession of the cod,
That held time, motionless, unknown to sound.

In bed at night,
Are his eyes open or is this a dream?
The room is all dark water, ghosted light,
And midway to the ceiling
The great fish with its working fins and gills
Suspended, while before it glide the reeling
And see-through scenes of day, faintly agleam,
Until their passage stills
And merges with the deep unmoving stream.

Oswald Spengler Watches the Sunset

The air is drenched with day, but one by one
      The flowers close on cue,
Obedient to the declining sun.
Forest and grasses, bush and leaf and stem,
They cannot move (and nor, you dream, can you);
      It is the wind that plays with them.
Only the little midges dancing still
      Against the evening move at will.

This tiny swarm still dancing on and on
      Like something in a net
Expanding and contracting, that late swan
Towing its wake, a solitary crow
Crossing the twilight in its silhouette,
      The fox proceeding sly and slow:
They are small worlds of purpose which infuse
      The world around with will to choose.

An animalcule in a drop of dew—
      And so diminutive
That if the human eye should look clear through
That globe there would be nothing there to see—
Although it only has a blink to live,
      Yet in the face of this is free;
The oak, in whose vast foliage this dot
      Hangs from a single leaf, is not.

The Music of What Happens

It is to this all art aspires,
They say,
When those twin helices, the double gyres
Of form and content turn as one instead,
Until whatever sense they may
Be said to have, though sensed, cannot be said.

And isn't that what happens here
From day
To day, this fashioning they engineer
Of time through time: the way the air arranges
The sky or makes the treetops sway,
Or washing wrestles with its shadow changes,

A thermal rises from the plain,
A wave
Crawls emptily and lets the sea remain,
An intricately moulded sheet of water,
Flung from a plastic pail to lave
The pavement by a neighbour's squealing daughter,

Casts a transparent, dimpled, belled,
Ruched, laced
And pleated arc, which almost seems upheld
Against its own liquidity and weight,
Then breaks, its shattered wetness traced
Like shadows, though they soon evaporate.

The Pictures

The kind of heat where Pan,
They say, might simply warp and twist
Out of the wrinkled air. On that rock shelf
At noon, though, no one stranger than
You two, self pressed to naked self,
While water wrinkled light across the sand.
Those shining slippery loops still net your wrist
And snag in shimmers on your upturned hand.

Or getting off the tram,
A smear on distant Castlereagh,
You stood beside your gloved and hatted mother,
An undeciphered pictogram
You'd almost take to be another
Ghosting that grainy footage. Those oblique
Projections, though you turn your head away,
Still flicker on the profile of your cheek.

What passed on the drowned lake
Swims in the focus of your eyes.
The bedroom shadows that your bitterest
And midnight insults made to quake
Lie mottled on your moving breast.
No need, no need to travel back so far
In search of incidents to authorize.
Simply collect yourself. Stay where you are.

No limb, no contoured part,
No pigment, pore, no pit behind
The joint, no swollen tissue that is you,
But wears the transfer of this art,
Its breathing temporal tattoo.
To think of all that desperate hue and cry;
All of the memories you went to find
Are you and now, that you now verify.

Precious Few

Not him. You've seen him by a garden bed,
Hard at it on his haunches with a trowel,
Though once the pink dome of his hairless head
Emerged above the fence,
And there with glistening eyes and wobbly jowl
And idle humour to dispense
He left you free to let five minutes lapse
While somewhere in the grounds his guinea fowl
Made cries like rusty taps.

But that won't do it. Certainly not her,
Above her boyfriend with her knees apart
And ardour which the broad day can't deter,
Sprawled in a public park
Among such seeding grass as Jeffrey Smart
Would paint, and over them that dark
Oppression behind the sky and garish city
He brings to bear. One day. And yet your heart
Is hardened against pity.

Nor even her. You scarcely would believe
Such indurated certainty. But no,
Not even her, met on her final eve,
And with her wasted frame
Depleted even from two months ago,
A rumour then who could not claim
Indulgence of your thoughts through half an hour.
Look how her daughters usher her as though
She held a precious power

The having and the loss of which they'll bear
Like some glass vessel brimming in the hand
Away with them. But you will not go there.
The dead with claim on you
Are elsewhere, and you're shocked to understand
In all the crying world how few.
One day. Then you will bear what must be borne.
And these will not turn back to reprimand
Your impotence to mourn.

The House of Time

And fleetingly it seemed to him
That in between one eye blink and the next
Time paused, allowing time to be installed
Within that countless interim,
Coiled up, on hold,
A memory predicted and recalled.
Now, that weak muscle flexed,
All that contained him started to unfold

In front of him, a moving book
In three dimensions he could wander through,
At will, at any point, now, since, before,
To feel, to listen and to look—
A house, or suite
Of rooms around a circling corridor,
And waiting there, he knew,
Were all the peopled days he'd not repeat.

Slowly he stretched his hand to open
The first door on his right. Why, this was easy:
Christmas when he was seven, and his aunt
Playing a polonaise by Chopin,
Badly. "Lenore,
We know you think you can, dear, but you can't."
And he was resting, queasy
From too much pudding. Now, another door:

So far, so faint, not yet an I,
A pulse of sense, he hung upon a web
Of knitted blood. Above, the muffled heart
Performed its mindless lullaby

And in the womb
He slept on half-awake. That was his part
Elsewhere, too, at the ebb
Of his last consciousness. Another room:

He recognized at once the face
Of one who five years hence he would have bound
As closely to him as a Siamese twin.
How recklessly he would replace
That loving care.
Absorbed, now, in the dream of skin on skin,
He whispered the profound
And destined promises she'd never share.

He shuddered, shut it, and proceeded.
So room on room, all of his scenes, arranged
In simultaneous succession, played
Before him, unignored, unheeded,
Each a *tableau*
Vivant and drama, driven and yet stayed,
Developing, unchanged.
At last the time that paused for time to flow

He saw was coming to an end.
He saw himself before himself, distinct
As when—a life ago—it came to him
A single blink could comprehend,
And then unfold,
All time within that countless interim.
He blinked. And then he blinked.
And time continued as it coiled, on hold.

Inarticulate

It's true the full impressionable weight
And placed articulation of those limbs
Are gone for good and only in the whims
Of dream and memory investigate
These retrospective chambers for the date
In which the foot is flexed, head turns, mouth prims
Before the compact mirror, gloved hand trims
The rose stems, tongue has fancies to relate.

But still among your clothes for a little while
In some few fully human cells will issue
The scent of you in the scent you would apply,
And in your purse, imprinted on a tissue,
Your red lips waiting in a folded smile
Will show themselves as lost for words as I.

Vertigo

All of their nights and days, then, are deleted,
Or so it seems,
Gone from the world, now that their time's completed,
Their hungers and their thirsts, the flush of passion
That compassed you as well perhaps and led
Briefly from here—except that in odd dreams
You will be visited,
Near dawn, say, when the window light is ashen.

Lying, you'll feel some settling of collapse
Deep in your sense
Of earthly certainty, as those slight gaps
Give way beneath the weight of what remains.
But then what does remain? Are not your own
Made of the same and failing elements?
That ringing telephone,
Of all the mornings that your life contains,

Wakes you on this. Climbing, in *Vertigo*,
Those phobic stairs,
James Stewart turns and gazes back below,
Hallucinating in the lower flights
Unreal and terrifying depths extended
Through those few feet. It seems that this day shares
That groundless view, suspended,
As on a landing, over all the nights

And days that form the staircase to its summit.
Downward you gaze,
Almost imagining that you could plummet
Right to the very bottom of that well
Of mounting time, in which is set in place
In all its living presence every day's
Dimension to embrace
Whatever you became there when you fell.

What if, as Russell joked, the world was made
Just now, with stores
Of memory placed within us to persuade
Belief in preterite fullness and past age—
Like that old notion that the Earth is young
But came with fossils of the dinosaurs
Compressed and slipped among
The pictures on its fresh, God-doctored page.

Saccade

They have no sense of what they're looking at,
Unless the object moves.
(Or so he's read; who knows if that's the case?)
A painted bird's an empty analogue
To the oblivious cat.
And it is not his still familiar face
So much as that distinctive gait which proves
The master to his dog,
Who frolics for him like an acrobat.

His eyes need movement too, but make their own.
His most fixated gaze—
On one small figure in a Bruegel scene,
Or on the camber of his lover's lip
He worships unbeknown,
As though no time or change will supervene—
Aflicker with saccade, adjusts and strays
Minutely to equip
His mind to take in what is being shown.

And maybe consciousness employs saccade
As well, and flickers back
And forth, now in the world, now, briefly, out—
The way the gum tree's canopy overhead
Flickers with light and shade,
So every leaf is momently in doubt—
Its faith saved by such intermittent lack
From being surfeited,
Its constant sense being constantly unmade.

Time Out

Only the trees perhaps, the sleeves of grass,
Leaning against the light, learn to compose
The windbent seconds as they pass
In cells of cellulose.

Or else the creatures in their quest to kill
And to survive, deliver or devour,
Stretch to its limit as they fill
The membrane of the hour.

But you, where *are* you in the falling day?
Some drowned god drags your foot off Sounion.
This quartet eats your heart away.
You stare, but the sky is gone.

Lost World

That roar, dragged by the vacuum it creates,
Swarms up the slope into the sky's
Exhausted limit, where a cottage waits.
The flames come rushing on, as tall
As office blocks. Dashed by the solar squall,
Trees thrash and, one by one, volatilize.

Paint bubbles from the walls. The rooms explode.
Fragments of melted window strafe
The lawn like wept and frozen tears. And stowed
These fifteen years in the garden shed,
Harry's old jacket flares from grey to red,
And burns to ash. So too the photograph

Slipped in an inside pocket. And now burns
As well another summer day
In 1935 among the ferns
Up on the mountain where she sat
And, smiling from beneath her broad-brimmed hat,
Made all the careless elements delay.

A little earlier, or in a while,
And a quite other face or pose
Might have been taken than this shadowed smile,
Which no one may have seen except
These two, the nameless and the dead, or kept
The curling memory of. And now, who knows?

How can we even say that scene took place?
Unless some wild surmise intrudes,
That what has been persists, a print in space—
Crushed fossil, drowned Minoan comb,
That burnt day—coded like a chromosome
With lost millennia and multitudes.

Selected Poems

Ulysses Burning

This room is the darkened theatre. Through the glass
The white veranda frames the stage
Like a proscenium. Garden, street and beach,
River and mountain, layer on layer, reach
Out to the backdrop of the sky
Before which all must pass that has to pass.

The river with its diamond-crusted gloss:
A Petri dish of gel in which
A culture of the sun is flourishing.
On the mountain, which aspires to Monet, cling
Veiled glares, some squeegee smears of cloud.
A creeper on the trellis hangs across

The wall of water, mountain, sky, as though
Its tendrils twined through them, as their
Confection oozes through the lattice squares.
Far out, one lone vermilion sailboard flares,
A soul whose punishment's to flee
The bliss he's riding on, who seems to slow

The vagrant eye to focus, or pulse on
The shuttered eyelid's blindness, less
Impelled to motion by the wind's weak force
Than by some fanciful odylic source;
Or simply, like a solar panel
Prompted with light, pushed by the moving sun.

I look. The people I take in take in
The view they partly constitute.
What here can last the longest? The mountain slopes
Vanish behind the glaze like fading hopes,
Lapsed concentration. The river burns
Away to a vapour. Prickings of a pin,

The glitter points are whiting out my sight.
Two couples amble by, and sun,
Firing the women's dresses, rouses me.
Like spirits out of Dante's *Comedy*
The walking flames sway past, their forms
Wrapped in a fabric of ignited light

Within which step their shadows. As they glide,
They still cling to the view, and I
To them, while brilliant day devours us, body
And sight. And though desire would make them tardy,
They must proceed towards the frame
And disappear as on a pushing tide.

On the river's silver terrace ride remote
Translucent sails of wind-slow yachts,
Combusting in this last declension of
The sun, in motion scarcely seen to move,
Like more of Dante's walking flames,
Ulysses burning, statically afloat.

The Secret Life of Books

They have their stratagems too, though they can't move.
They know their parts.
Like invalids long reconciled
To stillness, they do their work through others.
They have turned the world
To their own account by the twisting of hearts.

What do they have to say and how do they say it?
In the library
At night, or the sun room with its one
Curled thriller by the window, something
Is going on,
You may suspect, that you don't know of. Yet they

Need you. The time comes when you pick one up,
You who scoff
At determinism, the selfish gene.
Why this one? Look, already the blurb
Is drawing in
Some further text. The second paragraph

Calls for an atlas or a gazetteer;
That poem, spare
As a dead leaf's skeleton, coaxes
Your lexicon. Through you they speak
As through the sexes
A script is passed that lovers never hear.

They have you. In the end they have written you,
By the intrusion
Of their account of the world, so when
You come to think, to tell, to do,
You're caught between
Quotation marks, your heart's beat an allusion.

A Message from the Hills

The absence that is afternoon is filling
The house again, like a substance, a white noise
That wipes the details she would love to believe in;

She was taught to: the headlines with their mantras
Of event; the texture of those oranges
Whose tang anoints the fingertips; the windows

Of envelopes that keep remembering
Her name. Habit and memory, she murmurs,
Are all that hold this cup safe on the table.

The distant view of hills is almost merging
Into pale sky. It might be there the music
Is coming from. This is the crux: the singing

Distance with its lies of elsewhere, the landscape's
Absolute indifference to there or here.
Ibis rise from some gulf in the scenery

Like papers in a dust devil, then fly off
In purposeful ones or twos, like couriers
To a higher power bearing news that matters.

Chiaroscuro

1 Play of Light

Like butterflies refracted on the lawn
That scatter from view
Wind-wasted,
A swarm of sailboards prettifies the river,
Papery wings held stiff above their backs,
Out there, hundreds of yards,
So much confetti, I imagine, from
Above,
A festive excess left littering the water.
Now the estuary is matt
And grey,
Doing a perfect imitation of the sky
(That inverted river
Concocted out of cloud),
Two suspended widths of elephant hide.

But now the sun comes out, a flush of blue
Goes fleeing across
The surface
Like those abrupt and rapid colour changes
That flood across the skin of cuttlefish,
Flames of a radiant.
The sky must be auditioning all its
Effects

For a theatrical agent; bored with brilliance
It brings on rain, as weather tries
Its hand
At metalwork on water: pools of solder spill
Here and there, while deftly
Round them the verticals
Punch indentations in the river's plate.

Perhaps I am the agent.
I view all this behind a gauze, a scrim,
As from behind a delicate waterfall
That makes me want to wipe my eyes
Of something caught in them.
Pulling it back,
I zoom to focus like a lens, or that
First moment when,
Awake,
I put my glasses on.

What do they think of out there all day long?
I've scarcely had time
For breakfast
And morning's full of this air-shaped flotilla.
Late afternoon—no change, except the sun
Which, setting, x-rays them,
As it ignites in place of every sail
One flame.
This surely must be Keats's world of sensation
Rather than of thought, where they pour
Themselves
Into the skilful breeze's chiropractic, to
Muscles' fine adjustments,
A mind-free pleasuring
While all around them, look, the rich world burns.

Is this envy? I sit and read of deaths,
Then look up at them,
The men of
Action. But what and whose is action? Giving
Themselves so perfectly to now, the world's
Surface, in contact bliss
They're almost passive, while the faulted mind
Is flexed,
And exercised to the reach of its resources.
Even without the goblin-faced
Regard
Of the dead I have no wish to detach myself,
Who shall soon enough be
Windblown. Then let the scratch
Of thought mark silence like cat's claws on glass.

Now with a gust they scatter.
The day is like a time-lapse film where clouds
Build up their turbulent empires and decline.
Sparser and sparser as the sun
Dips, almost over now
The mountain's prop,
Their brilliants dulling upwards to the tips,
All day they strive
To be,
And will be, blown away.

2 Shadow Play

Man is a dream of a shadow

                                —Pindar

A sculpture of pure emptiness

                                —Paul Davies

Here, through the window's warp of glass, a pane
Of frozen space, the mountain hangs its slope,
Faint sweep of watercolour, a mauve stain,
Three brushstrokes from a miniature landscape
Which hardly differentiates between
The sky around it and the faded shape;
Having, in heat, no substance, no more real
Than shadow that floats about it like a veil.

Suddenly it's an engaging point of view.
The island's sombre permanence becomes
Less downright, less a cause to fall into
That sadness of the transitory which seems
To lie in wait for vistas, then, on cue,
Appear, as though—well, no, for shadow confirms—
The beautiful explicit world's no freer
From loss of its reality than we are.

Here and not here. Two books have this defined:
Mansfield Park and Davies' *Superforce*.
Reading from each in turn I feel my mind
Is dislocated. Austen's world of course

Does not know doubt. It is measured and designed
Like its estates and gardens, and assures
With rigid plans and reason, formally
Committed to this world's solidity.

In Davies' world of ghostly particles
We take the quantum leap; uncertainty
In Newton's classic universe prevails.
Abandon, not hope, but mere reality
All you who enter here, where everything calls
The bluff of common sense, where what you see,
What you observe, is all that is, and what
Is unseen can't be said to be or not

To be. If matter is charge, charge force, and force
A warping of space, then all creation's just
A frolic of convoluted nothingness,
Self-structured void determined to exist,
A blank coiled up into a universe.
So the truth is out. Not merely, dust to dust,
Do we proceed from nothing to nothing again,
But we're made up of nothing in between.

Well, most of politics is now explained,
And much of what has often passed for thought.
Should I be thrilled then or appalled? Too stunned
For either by the lesson I've been taught,
I have sudden new respect, I find,
For pavements, recalling *If on a Winter's Night*
A Traveller, where Calvino sees the earth
Go blank about him like a loss of faith.

I feel like—what?—like one of those entranced
Religious devotees who walk on coals
But are not burnt, whose backs and limbs are lanced
And pierced with eager hooks, though no blood falls,
When what is real is no longer sensed
And something that is not takes the controls.
In some way, it appears, sheer wilfulness
Or wishful thinking made the universe

Burst open like a flower, and it trembles
In the breeze of being, balanced like a chair
In that slow instant just before it tumbles
Forward or back: a floating world; in air,
In a breeze too slow to see, the mountain crimples
And peels like the flower hanging there,
Rocks swirl like petals into the blue day,
Cling for a moment and are blown away.

Reef

It is night. The spectrum has been cancelled
From the glossary of possibles. And here,
Its lettered spines a texture of the wall,

The library is restful as a morgue,
The horse's kingdom and Bezukhov's laugh
Quite notional—potential attributes

Remote from now as last year's holiday;
Inside the cabinet the compact discs,
Like objects of exotic sacrament,

Are clipped inert in cases, as far from song
As the cat before the fire from algebra;
Amnesia has effaced this photograph:

Memento mori like the chunk of coral
Beside the portrait on the mantelpiece,
An exoskeleton tonight unnamed

By colour, as once it was unnamable.
They are waiting for the time and hand of need.
They are waiting for the howl of memory.

Once in that grip they'll take their colours back,
Plunged in a brilliant polyhedral sea,
A sliding light. Here again is the view

Through the glass-bottomed boat, the exorbitant
Forms of the fishes, the walk upon the reef,
The reckless leg laid open to the bone.

The Sail and the Gannet

A single sail,
Translucent apricot,
Drifts like a poppy's petal on a frail
Breeze that is not—

A baby's breath
Of air sparingly strewn
And eked out by the estuary's width
All afternoon.

Lit from behind,
That fabric puts on show
What all of this, when the sun has declined,
Will undergo,

When like a dye
Extravagantly loosed,
Late saffron through blue river and blue sky
Will be suffused.

Hours that require
Only themselves. Suspended,
Division and the eye dissolve, desire
Almost is mended.

The close of day
Approaches: echelons
Of shade and light ascend the river, grey
And flooded bronze.

That sail's no more.
And out of nowhere looms
One gannet, sweeping up and down the shore,
In the gold glooms

Seeking the day's
Last fish. So swift it flies
And circles and returns, rushing to appraise
What underlies

Its beat, it brings
A darker note into
The scene, as though to match the darkenings
That drain the view.

Too fast its flight
(And slightly desperate
Before the urgings of the loss of light)
To concentrate

Its faculties
On fish, it can't be seeing,
You feel—or it's this shadowing it sees,
And is now fleeing.

The Last Day

The process still unspools, perversely normal,
Like stubble on the chin of a dying man.
Surely, this has to be that perpetual-

Motion machine, the crackpot patent-seekers'
Cherished chimera, that nothing will perturb
Or knock from course: there swell and elongate

The evening clouds, a film of amoebic life
In a waterdrop; there sinks, word-perfect,
The professional sun behind its bodyguard

Of elms and stone façades, as little able
As any other actor in the piece
To see beyond the context of the plot,

Or step down from the screen, extempore
Among the terrors.
                              But still, all afternoon,
A pale light floods the café wall through glass,

As though through water, in which all these couples
And their drowning intimacies take on
The sadness of their folly, and into

The gold lips of the coffee cups, the plates,
The wrist-defying silver cutlery,
The fat cream pooled in jugs, the too rich cakes,

The *moues*, the probably clever chat, contracts
And gathers vastly, like a collapsing star,
The gravity of their lives, an age, a culture.

The trees flex in the wind, as hitherto,
Arranging their shed leaves for another place—
Paris, perhaps, in 1923.

The cut-out treasury still poses for
Tonight's performance, as usual so polished
That applause would be *de trop*.
                                        In some apartment

Elsewhere, the cut thumb, even, of a housewife
At the sink, after the water's blush has washed
Away, and all she's left with is a throb

There like a pulse, even that domestic thumb
Will quietly, unstoppably start to heal
Under the motherly kiss of the grand assumption.

Diversions of a Painter

Las Meninas by Velázquez

Near right, the dwarf Nicolasito
Prods to arouse with his black shoe's
Diminutive and cheeky veto
The mastiff which would sooner snooze.
Next to him, quaintly beatific,
Eyes fixed on some unseen, specific
Point of focus, the squat buffoon
Maribárbola stands immune
To her surroundings. On the left hand,
Before a canvas turned from view,
The artist is included too,
Absorbed in observation, deft hand
Poised with a ready brush to set
Down—what? We do not know as yet.

Mid-foreground, pert with inattention
But still prepared to acquiesce
In this elaborate invention,
Is posed the five-year-old princess,
The setting's dainty prima donna.
On either side, a maid of honour:
One knelt in tender protocol;
One tilted like a lifeless doll.
On the back wall what seems a painting
(Of king and queen?), alone among
The canvases which there are hung
In shadow, gleams distinctly. Tainting
With day the intimate half-gloom
Which stills that quarter of the room,

An open door presents its splendid
Oblong of light and, watching there,
A chamberlain is held suspended
With fascination on the stair.
The room seems spacious, only cluttered
By these few figures. They have shuttered
All but two windows on the right
Which shed their glow just out of sight.
Behind the doll-like maid a pair of
Superfluous attendants stand—
She, with turned face and gestured hand,
Prattling to him, quite unaware of
Her station. He, oblivious,
Stares at the canvas closed to us.

What is the painting in the painting,
If we could peep around the frame?
What subject was Velázquez feinting
In playing this reflexive game?
In one sense, nothing, for quite clearly,
The work within the work is merely
The canvas back and frame we see.
The full front is a fantasy.
As meaningless to pose the question
As ask what Hamlet might have done
Or said three days before Act One;
As fanciful as the suggestion
A living person could declare
That he is Don Quixote's heir.

But art begins here to bamboozle.
What seemed a portrait on the wall
At first glance is, on close perusal,
Really a mirror after all.
The silvered king and queen, detected
In glass, turn out to be reflected
From that position where they pose
Beyond the scene the picture shows.
That canvas, then, is their depiction?
So it is they the small princess
And Maribárbola address?
Well, no; this is another fiction.
Those mirror images depict
No couple, but the viewer tricked.

And now you see his game, his clever
Subversion of the paradigm.
He's playing with you, viewer, whoever
You are, or where, or in what time.
He's almost starting to unnerve you,
For aren't you placed within his purview
Precisely where the subject is?
It's you that hooded gaze of his,
Standing back from the work, assesses
Within the work, or turns towards.
It's you the portraitist records.
You're the buffoon's and the princess's
Focus. Found out through time, you're brought
To notice in the Spanish court.

Enough, though, of these artful cruces.
How did he really paint the thing?
Mirrors may answer many uses.
He placed one where the questioning
Spectator stands, in which reflexion
The room lay bare to his inspection:
Dog, dwarfs, princess, maids, chamberlain
Arrested and entranced within
His block of light, and, there to haunt us,
Velázquez too, brush poised before
An edge of frame. But there is more.
The ghost of mirrors comes to haunt us
Now, for the picture that, we know,
Is in the picture has on show

Another easel (and a painter,
Dog, dwarfs, princess, maids, chamberlain,
Servants) which has a picture—fainter
Smaller—which has an easel, in
A spiral traced through time and distance
With its grotesque counterexistence.
Around each corner of a frame
You'll be confronted by the same,
Chasing Velázquez from this idyll
Of courtly life beyond the rhyme
Of reason, beyond eye and time.
(The only way to solve the riddle,
Cut short the regress, end the doubt?
Reach in and drag that canvas out.)

Penshurst

Sometimes we'd wander half-day holidays
Licensed as in a dream to roam at large,
Through afternoons of Empire Days, or those

More mundane times when we'd wag school, a friend
And I, and ramble home circuitously,
Traipsing the mid-hours of the suburbs, when

They'd sunk into their fabled lifelessness,
The great Australian emptiness: the men
Away at work, the faceless wives indoors,

Possessed by their invisibility,
Streets in suspense, deserted like a scene
From *The Quiet Earth*, apart from some roused dog,

The grace notes of the birds, mad Geiger-counting
Of cicadas (it seems always summer),
A Hill's hoist thinly shrieking, and hidden away

Somewhere behind the streets the intermittent,
Companionable clatter of the trains—
That rataplan I'd often lie in awake to

Late in the night in bed, muffled far off,
A goods train from the south that never seemed
To arrive, pass or recede, but simply hung

Its soporific rhythm's interminable
Comfort across the wide deceptive miles—
And the reassuring weight of houses, safe,

Repeated like a children's story, always
The same, their modest privacies behind
Net curtains intimately suggestible,

Indifferent; and all of it so far
From any need to happen or explain,
Be puzzled over or be otherwise.

The Menger Sponge

God made everything out of nothing; but the nothing shows through
                                    —Paul Valéry

Lost from all angles but the sun's,
This woken morning,
It clicks its brilliance into place at once,
If you follow the fall of light—
A spider web, head-high, adorning
The woodshed's entrance like a sheet
Of gold-shot fabric, metal-tight,
That, even so, one handswipe could delete,
Collapsing all
That spacious architecture to a tacky ball.

It brings to mind the mathematician's
Monstrous idea,
The Menger sponge, where infinite excisions
Out of a solid cube delete
Its substance while its form stays clear:
The central ninth is cut from a square;
Eight smaller squares remain; repeat
For each; and so on with this lattice of air:
A formula
For zero volume, infinite surface area.

Enough. The estuary's slung
Like gold-shot cloth
Over a gulf of shifting airs. Among
Cloud-drifts of beaten eggwhite floats,
As though confected of such froth,
The mountain. Like a Chinese screen,
The fabric of the view devotes
Almost all blankness to this hanging scene,
This one handsweep
Of water, creased like the cheek of someone roused from sleep.

The Complete Works

Over the city's basin, clouds progress:
Continents, Himalayas which bear down
Tectonic force, then evanesce;
Iguaçu Falls
Of turbulent dark marble which would drown
Oblivious dreamers in their flimsy walls,
But lack the gravity of their excess

And are shrugged off by foothills. One immense
Atomic tree form lifts its roiling bole,
Gripping the roofs of residence
It blows asunder,
While in its canopy tumble and roll
The smithereens of suburbs which lie under
That swelling umbrage: world-ash in either sense.

Such scenes of life and death—all make-believe,
An atmospheric horseplay flung together
That fifteen minutes can't retrieve.
The elements
Don't know their elements. They make bad weather.
A wind from nowhere just as soon invents
The evening's empty, lemon-lit reprieve.

Here by the window in the fuchsia's top,
A little wattlebird hangs, acrobatic,
Whose feathered tongue-tip probes to mop
The silly drug
Of its high spirits up. With instamatic
Eyes, it keeps taking snaps, the shutterbug,
Of fantasies that drift and rise and drop

Within the surface of that doubtful mirror:
The marbled sky's distant and vague champaign,
The see-through garden and this clearer
Twin; or it pores
On what the window's stranger deeps contain—
A figure drowning in interiors
Who sometimes floats up menacingly nearer.

What can it know of the image which adheres
To a page inside a book on that man's shelf
(Its own image, so it appears)
Which can attest
More detailed knowledge than the bird itself
Of where and what it is? Who could have guessed
This world it's flying through was once Shakespeare's?

Now fast within themselves the couples lie,
While through this autumn night the lightless cloud
Above their beds breeds in the sky
Vast Yggdrasils,
And earthly trees in darkness, bird-endowed,
Attempt to memorize a wind that spills
From the salt water, making the same cry.

What can they know, as pictures and remarks
Seed in their heads, occasionally to flower
In a dark endearment, or the quirks
Of eye and limb,
About their bodies' other plans, the power
That writes their names, their hidden homonym,
Simple as clouds and birds, complete as Shakespeare's works.

Contents Page

The jungle, from the floor to the canopy,
       Clogs and entwines
Its every rung and level with rank growth.
       The python dines
Among an epiphytic gaudery
       And hungry vines.
On the mizzled hair of the two-toed sloth
       Moss has designs.
Yet all that climbing tonnage is content-free.
The top limbs sway as though to write in air,
But can't remember what they scribble there.

Through the savanna's heat-glaze the herds pause,
       Ripple and shiver,
Or graze hypnotically, or drop their young,
       Which may deliver
Their wet thin steps into the lion's jaws.
       By pool or river
They stoop at evening side by side among
       The surface quiver
Of their reflexions as the light withdraws:
A fable set down in invisible ink;
They print their shadows on the pool they drink.

Even the perfect pictures in the shale's
       Slow-motion traps,
The filamentous feathers, which one or two
       Sharp hammer taps
Release, the fish in their meticulous scales,

The precise maps
Of leaves, did not direct this rendezvous.
    They're simply gaps
In time, and have no part in these details.
The weird wiwaxias, worms and arthropods
Were empty of intention as stone gods.

Once, though, a figure had the thought to crawl
        Out of the day
Into a cave's dark reach, its first invoker,
        And there to splay
His hand against the tallow-glimmered wall,
        And pause to spray
His mouth's cargo of spittle and red ochre
        On the array
Of his five fingers, clear, indelible:
Author and content of the space displayed,
The maker's hand becoming what it made.

Incident at Grantley Manor

Seven o'clock, the time set in his mind
Like herbs displayed in aspic, as the chimes
Were striking. Then the squeaking of his shoes'

Black leather tread, pacing those measures down
The first-floor hall, where sunset's apricot
Was oozing nectar through the open doors.

Her voice, conspiratorial and astonished,
Called him across the bedroom's drowning cube
Towards the window. How well Miss Waterson

Remembers it: "Please come and look at this,
Mr Devine;" the clock on the mantelpiece
Rehearsing for the hour of seven. She pointed

Down. There, a moving picture on the lawn,
His father, like a patient whose long months
Of immobility meant learning afresh

The art of walking, climbing the light's green slope
Towards the summer house, looking intently
As though for a cuff link or a signature.

That evening he still thinks of, lying now,
No longer needing lessons for his legs,
How he cast back his glance and saw the windows

Blazing like cats' eyes on his uselessness,
And in that golden mirror, two gold figures
Recording him, two shadows of dark gold—

Miss Waterson (was it?) and another one—
And then took out his watch on which the hands
Were so meticulously assembling seven.

Young Emily, appointed just the week
Before, came rushing to the stairs—she'd seen
Him stumble—to advise Mr Devine

About his father's fall. And so, almost
Immobilized herself in that clinging syrup,
She observed the hall clock's quaint rendition of

Seven, the time set clearly in his mind
Like summer herbs in aspic, as the chimes
Were striking. Then the squeaking of his shoes'

Black leather tread, pacing those measures down
The corridor, where sunset's apricot
Was oozing nectar through the open doors.

Her voice, companionable but astonished,
Floated across the bedroom's drowning cube
As he descended. How well Miss Waterson

Remembers it: "Please come and look at this;"
And Emily, who had just been taken on
That week, came rushing to the window. She pointed

Down, smartly on the stroke of seven. There,
A moving picture on the lawn, was old
Mr Devine, like a patient whose long months

Of immobility meant learning afresh
The art of walking, climbing the light's green slope
Abstractedly towards the rose garden.

That evening he still thinks of, lying now,
No longer needing lessons for his legs,
How he cast back his glance and saw the windows

Glaring like cats' eyes on his helplessness,
And in that golden mirror, two gold figures
Gesticulating, two shadows of dark gold—

The new girl (was it?) and another one—
And then took out his watch on which the hands
Were so laboriously assembling seven.

Miss Waterson, with Emily behind her
In a panic, dashed to the stairs to find
Mr Devine, anxious to let him know

About his father's fall. And there they saw him,
Almost immobile in that clinging syrup,
And heard the hall clock's muffled tolling of

Seven, the time set firmly in his mind...

Silk Screen

Furnished across a table,
The long provisions of midafternoon:
The cups, according as each tongue is able
To stand the heat, more or less full, and strewn
About a slewed and wrinkled
Expanse of damask that is crumb-besprinkled

With biscuit, scone and cake,
Freighted with plates and variously stained.
A gathering suffused with the slight ache
Of an old familial boredom, unexplained,
Transacted intimately.
Behind the group the windowed estuary,

Which until now had been
Delayed among such subtleties as those
Played out inside, too dull to make a scene,
Emerges from its featureless repose.
Now as the winter light
Sinks yet one more degree into respite,

Its talcum powder greys,
Ranked far towards the city, screen on screen,
Bewitchingly detain what they erase,
Assembling a new scene from the unseen,
So that the pooled and pleated
Spread of river, tree stencils, mist-deleted

Bluffs and bays, the tiers
Of suburbs from the foreshore's basque of foam
Up to the foothills—everything inheres
Ghosted behind a wash of monochrome.
A shadow light invades
Cloud, water, slopes: so many Chinese grades

Of columbine and pearl,
Layered against a parquetry of pewter,
Gunmetal plates and sheets of faded merle.
Uncolours lost to colour, rendered neuter
(A glintless skyey sheen
Of eau de nil that is bankrupt of green,

A Copenhagen blue
Deprived of blue), obsessing concentration
By drawing each declared outline and hue
Into a hushed grisaille of intimation.
Through mantling of matt silk
Seeps a pine rumour. Drowned in shadowed milk,

Loomings ride up and swim
Of breath-faint hulls and mastheads. Over there on
The docks, some gantry stain behind the scrim
Stands groping. Steeped in day, a half-guessed heron
Silently intercedes
Among the lead-lit shallows where it feeds.

And now, melting as if
Oozed from the river's deep to its bleared bank,
One solitary blush mark, a rose gliff
Of sun, escapes the cloud on the mountain's flank
And instantly instils
A drop of dye that quickens where it spills.

Absorbed into the screen
They're ranged against, the figures face to face,
Sipping and mumbling cake, chatting between
Mouthfuls, become still shadows at its base
To at least one pair of eyes,
For which the window mounts its final guise.

The sun cannot resist
Showing the flag of imperial Japan
(Except translucent, moted with the mist),
Whose bars of apricot and salmon fan
That band of liquor which
Their deepening audacities enrich.

The river's ash and nacre
Are flooded where the crimsons grow across,
And as those figures dim to simulacra
Tableaued in black, the screen redeems its loss,
Ransoming in red
The colours afternoon had forfeited.

The Shadow Maker

Faded long since into the shadow world,
He has their measure by the light of day—
That talent which the child would claim,
To grab the plait of water as it dangles
Down from the tap (no game),
Or snatch at rainbow splashes or the spangles
Scattered by a sun-twirled
Bauble on a wall (but they won't obey).

He is the one who skims the roughened shade
Of an oak that sprawls the lawn's green continent
(A ghostly Gulliver), and plucks
One at a time its flickering rags of leaves,
All muzzy in the flux
Of glare, with weightless effort he retrieves
A skirt's black escapade
Along the pavement, stoops to the descent,

Click and upliftment of a heel, purloining
The foot's dark double as it's printed there.
He peels from doorways, shopfront glass,
Walls, car flanks, fences, limbs and profiles, second
By second as they pass,
The generation, various and fecund
As what we find adjoining
Us in mirrors, of the shadow world we wear.

Away from here, beyond the sun's bright sway,
He draws out and prolongs their otherwise
Impossible unbeing, weaves
Their unsubstantial fashion into nets,
The rippling negatives
Of gauze-fed gonfalons and bannerettes
He shakes out in display.
Undaunted by the daylit enterprise,

He flourishes his silhouettes in mesh
Between us as we breathe in and exhale,
Trawling among the looks we share,
These mouths, the working of our limbs, between
Our silvered bodies where
At length they lie engaged, still hungry in
The fable of the flesh,
And in our eyes, briefly, the colours fail.

Midas

Not literally gold—the apple plucked,
And in that gilded gesture not just weighing
His palm down with its glittering bullion, but
Crisping too from the severed stem, its sap
Already foil, back up and up the branch
An aureate rust, or frost, until the tree
Entire shook shimmering under the breeze
And tinkled like a fragile instrument;
The rich brocades become tautologous
As under his evaluative caress
The fabric took contagion from the pattern's
Colour and substance, stiffening, as though
He braced in his aching arm a loved one's corpse;
Indeed, his little daughter, when he bent
To kiss her lineless forehead with its dew
Of sleep, instantly goosefleshed with chill beads
Of priceless gold, less precious, though, than she
They took possession of, while all the tears
He shed were alchemized and stilled at once
Across her cheeks—not literally gold:

His granted wish, though, brought him all desire
Could ever catalogue or, in the mind's
Disreputable theatre, clothe in form,
So that, before his eyes, materialized,
Like mist condensing into solid flesh,
Or fruit or fabric, metal, adamant,
Or carven marble, ivory, ebony,
Whatever shape and style his fancy chose.
Just simple things at first, say a gold ring
(For, after all, the leitmotiv of gold

Had to have sprung from somewhere), only to test,
And disbelievingly confirm, the gift
He was not yet persuaded of; a sceptre
Sapphire crusted; a sword so damascened
And so enchased a shield, that to have used
Their virtues in the arbitrament of arms
Would seem a sacrilege; exotic stuffs,
Rare and unheard-of spices, unguents, scents.
Then living lusts, of course, did not escape
Instant induction to his treasury:
A falcon jessed in silk; a jet-black stallion;
A snow leopard that purred as his palm roved
Over her jaspé flank, and from his lap
Half-raised her head to yawn and flex one paw;
A room of blinded nightingales to cool
Noon's stifled lull with midnight song; and then,
Companions too to ease those other fires
Which casually flared and sought release
In ever changing lineaments, new eyes,
New pastimes of the tongue, received and given,
Languid entanglements of stranger limbs.

But soon he saw how irresistibly
His gift was drawn to subtler consummations;
Less physical, more nuanced categories
Of mental practice were hypostatized:
Whatever longing, hope, imagined need,
Whatever aspiration of the spirit,
Or of the heart, not merely of the flesh,
Whatever goal or appetite of will,
From firm intent down through volition's ranks
To the pallid spectres of velleity—
Out of his brain they teemed and poured, assuming
Extraordinary shapes as he looked on,
Dream figurations which, in normal dreams,

Dawn would undo, but here gave substance to
And set them up among the furnishings.
And gradually it became apparent
That his mind and sense, so overloaded and
Dispersed through this profusion, could not sustain
Sufficient interest in each single item
To keep it fresh, infused with pristine charm.
The objects dulled and hardened, and the casts
Of gynaeceum and menagerie
Ground to a lifeless halt, until his chambers
Were less a king's extravagant abode
Than a dead tyrant's tomb, freighted with all
The futile requisites of the afterlife,
Or some collector's basement, crammed to the cornice
With bits and pieces of his fetish, once
Not to be done without, but useless now,
Locked from his life, even his memory.

And truly it was out of him they came—
Too soon not at his bidding, precisely where
And when and how he wished each one to tease
The nerve of his delight, but ever more
Autonomous, unchecked, incontinent.
At last his brain scarcely belonged to him.
And unlike love, which grows on its expense,
This generation of still-breeding thoughts
Depleted him, so imperceptibly
At first that his lightheadedness seemed less
A kind of faintness than intoxication.
But when the lightness spread (in much the way
The gold infection of the myth is shown)
From one point to the whole, like dye in water,
His body then was weakened with a fatigue
Whereby the lifting of a foot, the hand's
Extension to a stylus or his beard,

Even the mouth's laborious arrangements
To shape the weightless air into empty words,
The very mind's exertion to raise up
The phantoms of its process, proved too hard.
Leaning against some bulk of luxury,
Too weary for disgust, still more despair,
He sat, transparent to the sunlit breeze
That nudged him from the window thoughtlessly,
One with the shifting robes that gave him form.

Sun Pictorial

How formal and polite,
How grave they look, burdened with earnest thoughts,
In all these set-up sepia stills,
Almost as if, embarrassed and contrite
To be caught practising their fatal skills,
They'd stepped aside from slaughter for these other shots.

The American Civil War,
The first war captured by the photograph
In real time. Even the dead
Seem somehow decorous, less to deplore
The sump of blood to which their duty bled
Than to apologize, humbled, in our behalf.

We know how otherwise
It was. They knew it then. The gauche onset
Of murderously clumsy troops,
Dismemberment by cannon, the blown cries
Through powder smoke, mayhem of scattered groups
In close engagement's pointblank aim and bayonet.

How far from then we've come.
The beauties of the Baghdad night still stun
Me: a blue screen where guns and jets
Unloose the lightnings of imperium—
Intense enough to challenge a minaret's
Aquamarine mosaic in the blinded sun

At noon—and smart bombs fall
Through walls to wipe the city street by street.
Morning, and in the camera's light
The formal corpses ripen. Who can recall
By day precisely what they watched last night?
Or find the unknown soldier in a field of wheat?

Being surplus, like the killed,
Millions of those old plates were simply dumped.
And in a modern version of "swords
To ploughshares", many were reused to build
Greenhouses, ranged and set in place as wards
Above the rife tomatoes as they blushed and plumped,

While, through the daily sun's
Pictorial walls and roofs, the long, desired,
Leaf-fattening light fell down, to pore
Upon the portraits of these veterans
Until their ordered histories of the war
Were wiped to just clear glass and what the crops transpired.

Elemental

in loving memory of Ann Jennings

The body's graces which you graced
Are irretrievably effaced,
And all you were that now is not,
And will no more, resolves to what
These gathered memories can make
From shreds of pleasure and heartache.
The lines around your eyes and lips,
The gestures of your fingertips,
Those limbs that love moved and desire
Are disembodied now like fire.

The living graces which you graced
By the vast future are displaced:
That long and windy corridor
Echoing many, but no more
One who for years had seemed to be
The purpose of chronology.
Breath that your throat and mouth gave shape
And meaning to must now escape
With its inhuman sense to share
The passage of the griefless air.

The troubled graces which you graced
Are passed from turmoil now and haste;
And as a stormswept landscape will
Appear when the blown lake grows still
And seem more piercing, even clearer,

Viewed in that unsubstantial mirror,
So, when the elements relent
That left your image racked and bent,
You will come clear, clear but remoter
Than the light's pictures in the water.

The day's lent graces which you graced,
Called back into the night's dead waste,
In absence, loss and negative
Keep even so their power to give
And teach us the unmaking of
All works except the works of love.
And your withdrawing hands which slip
The failing outreach of our grip,
Your memory-engraven face
Which memory must now replace,
Leave us, and leaving us impart
Your beauty, courage, strength of heart,
While you, released at last from pain,
Content perhaps that we retain
These riches fashioned out of dearth,
Sink weightless to the waiting earth.

The Immortals

A breeze fills up the manna gum's huge lung,
That hologram of bronchioles. It sways there
Tethered and shifting like a hot-air balloon
Preparing for some fresh and doomed attempt
To circle the great globe. Heaped at its base
The litter of shed bark and collapsed boughs,
So much dumped ballast. Across an expanse of lawn—
The cat's savanna—a drowsing figure slouched
In an easy chair inhabits "Summertime",
Living by emptying this gap of day:
A straw hat on her face like a cartoon peon,
Her right arm limply draped over the side,
Jehovah's index finger pointing down
To where, half lost in the long grass, Daniel
Deronda's lying in *Daniel Deronda*,
His pages palping at the air, as though
Blindly taking in what it all is like.

It *is* hard to imagine. The shallow bay
Offers up to the light the illusory depths
Of a table buffed and polished to a lustre,
Except where an inlet-wide, flung net of wind
Hauls at the panicked shoals of chop and dazzle.
High up the sky is pale as faded denim
Worn through in a few frayed clouds, but where it comes

To earth, a cyan heavier than air
And not to breathe. And sometimes in the evening
The whole space thinks again, and sky and sea
Lie in each other's mirror, robed in gold
And self-absorbed against the envious land
They leach away, but for some failing islet
Or bluff that barely makes its presence felt.

Look, on her hand's back are the clues to grief,
Whatever she may think—those patches like
The remnants of a suntan, veins as blue
As any sky could wish, swollen through skin
As beautiful as birch bark, and as frail—
The emblems of a loss that will see out
The ending of the world.

Persisting in some region of obtuse
Sublimity, and full of an inhuman,
Distant pity, he'll contemplate her, baffled,
Then turn away perhaps like Beatrice
With her doubt-tainted smile. But he'll be there.

The heat is a dimension now, like time,
And as improbable. The cottage floats,
Not quite convinced it's happening, with its flies
And cracked linoleum, its shelves of books
Unaltered since the war, its bush-rat droppings,
The clocklike clicking of the roof—all tethered
To the least twitching of her dreaming fingers,
Her shallow breath. Later, before her friends
Descend, she'll wander barefoot through the rooms
In something easy with an ice-filled glass
And put some music on and watch the sea.

Man on the Moon

Hardly a feature in the evening sky
As yet—near the horizon the cold glow
Of rose and mauve which, as you look on high,
Deepens to Giotto's dream of indigo.

Hardly a star as yet. And then that frail
Sliver of moon like a thin peel of soap
Gouged by a nail, or the paring of a nail:
Slender enough repository of hope.

There was no lack of hope when thirty-five
Full years ago they sent up the *Apollo*—
Two thirds of all the years I've been alive.
They let us out of school, so we could follow

The broadcast of that memorable scene,
Crouching in Mr Langshaw's tiny flat,
The whole class huddled round the TV screen.
There's not much chance, then, of forgetting that.

And for the first time ever I think now,
As though it were a memory, that you
Were in the world then and alive, and how
Down time's long labyrinthine avenue

Eventually you'd bring yourself to me,
With no excessive haste and none too soon—
As memorable in my history
As that small step for man onto the moon.

How pitiful and inveterate the way
We view the paths by which our lives descended
From the far past down to the present day
And fancy those contingencies intended,

A secret destiny planned in advance
Where what is done is as it must be done
For us alone. When really it's all chance
And the special one might have been anyone.

The paths that I imagined to have come
Together and for good have simply crossed
And carried on. And that delirium
We found is cold and sober now and lost.

The crescent moon, to quote myself, lies back,
A radiotelescope propped to receive
The signals of the circling zodiac.
I send my thoughts up, wishing to believe

That they might strike the moon and be transferred
To where you are and find or join your own.
Don't smile. I know the notion is absurd,
And everything I think, I think alone.

Eighth Heaven

I open the flyscreen door and slip inside,
Easing it shut. Low voices—the radio?—
Drift from the dining room, although their words

Are indistinct. A milky sort of light
Clings to the ceiling, showing that the summer
Is well established here and the inner shadows,

However cool they may appear, are tacky
As bare thighs on a vinyl chair.
My mother, at the kitchen bench, is pouring

Afternoon tea, or would be, but I see
That, unsurprisingly, that red-brown ribbon
Is stationary and the steam hangs still,

A Lilliputian fog. Can time have stopped
So simply, in this simple suburb, at
This hour of day? And yet the radio

Is lit up and those voices natter on,
Talking the timeless issues of the day
And advertising their predated products.

The sideboard stands, as ever, well equipped
With seldom used utensils, special service:
The special teapot of white china, capped

With shining metal like a soldier's casque;
The little glasses with their Chinese figures—
Sum Fun Tu, Me Fun Tu, Tu Yung Tu…; plates

Of many colours with their hidden names,
Remembering far better than I can
Their few occasions. And there is my father

Standing in the lounge room, half-turned away.
I summon up some greeting and can feel
The words unbodied, though not a sound disturbs

The house's depth. I walk in and am baffled
To find, however much I move about him,
That that one aspect is still turned to me,

Unmoving, a one-sided hologram.
Net curtains billow at the window, frozen
In air, as though a child were crouched in them.

In the middle of the wall the oval mirror
Declines to represent me, though I come
So close my breath appears on it. I place

My right hand's fingertips against the glass
And feel the surface tension of a pool
Resisting, then reluctantly giving in.

My fingers come away with silvered ends
Which, as they sway, show scraps of furniture
And carpet, flowers in a vase.

Now I am gazing out across the park.
The afternoon is caught among the leaves,
Detained indefinitely out there, and in

My throat. My fingers are still wet from touching
The glass; I must have brushed them on my cheek.
At the back gate I see that I am leaving:

That is my arm there sliding the bolt shut.
A bowl of fruit is on a table by
A window. On the round face of an apple

Surmounting it is held the light of the world.
It sits there like a globe of crystal, or
A painted droplet—the Earth that Dante saw

When he looked down at last from the eighth heaven.
Within it, sworn to secrecy, flamboyant,
Swim all the ages and the hours.

Living Colour

Out of Herr Feierabend's private vault
A stock of long lost film has finally come
To light, from that last summer before the War—
In colour too,
As bright and vivid as delirium.
It seems a kind of fault
In history and nature to restore
This Munich, underneath the flawless blue

Of mid-July in nineteen thirty-nine,
This pageantry of party-coloured kitsch.
The Fuehrer, with his bored assessing gaze,
And his gang, all braid
And frogging, leather-bound and medal-rich,
Sit large as life, benign
As the broad daylight, to accept like praise
The weather and the crowd and the parade.

Why should this hit me like a culture shock?
Just as the poet said she'd thought her home,
The blessed city, till she was born to bless it,
Had not known colour,
But lingered in prenatal monochrome,
So is the Nazis' stock
Portrayal, when the mind turns to address it,
All black and white, the greys of death and dolour.

The goose-step chorus line kicking at nothing,
With heads ricked to one side, where he looks on,
Torch-haunted rallies conjuring the tribe,
The pavements lined
With adoration's awful unison;
And the corpses piled like clothing,
Those gates that Dante thought to superscribe
Long since: all drained of colour in the mind.

But here in garish dress coat Goering draws
His decorations up to execute
Some greeting; there's Streicher smiling in the lens
Flushed and appalling;
And Hitler's there, giving his strange salute,
That stop sign to applause
Which calls up more. And as the arm unbends,
We see his pink cold fingers curl in falling.

Now past they flow, the floats and staged effects,
The gilded eagles, banners, fancy dress,
Teutonic warriors and virgins with
Blond streaming hair
(Who seem to tempt the heart to acquiesce
In what judgement rejects),
Like something spawned by Metro-Goldwyn-Mayer,
A figment spun from myth
Alive and beating in the gas-blue air.

Im Sommerwind

On a hot listless Sunday afternoon
I'm sprawling on the porch by the front door
While someone's radio murmurs a tune.

My mother's brought a chair out to maroon
Herself a moment between chore and chore
On a hot listless Sunday afternoon.

The screen door wants to let the house commune
With languid airs that stray in to explore,
While someone's radio murmurs a tune

That never seems to end or change, a croon
I can't attend to and don't quite ignore.
On a hot listless Sunday afternoon

Across the faded park figures are strewn,
Poised in the motives they have come here for.
While someone's radio murmurs a tune

Nothing can happen here, nothing impugn
The hour. It will be now for evermore
On a hot listless Sunday afternoon
While someone's radio murmurs a tune.

Summer

A spiritless, grey-lit interior,
Midafternoon, the nadir of the day
When visitors are scarce; as in a mime
Silence informs the empty corridor,
Making all sound extraneous, far away,
As though it were the memory of time:

A closing lift, a nurse's wordless voice
Monologizing on the office phone
Offscreen, the metal rattle of a trolley
With all it offers those without a choice,
And somewhere hard to judge the sullen drone
Of a polisher spreading its melancholy.

Wards open to the left and right, from which
The stillness wells like stage mist. Ranged in beds
Lie figures from the London underground
By Henry Moore, while in a curtained niche
An intimate family group with half-bowed heads
Out of Renaissance art sits gathered round.

As in a nightmare loop the eye regards
The bowls of grapes, the bunches of bright flowers
(Watered by someone once who then ignored them),
The drinking vessels and the get-well cards
Again, again the faces drained of hours,
Emptied by their waiting even of boredom,

Subsisting in their realm of four o'clock.
Procedure rooms pass by, and linen stores,
And stores for dressings, cannulas, syringes,
And blank, shut rooms where no one comes to knock.
Glimpsed from a junction in the corridors
What seems a painting down the hall impinges

Into the atmosphere, although the glare
That pullulates across it from the lighting
Wipes out its subject from the dazed newcomer,
Till he approaches closer to that square
Of tell-tale glass, which stares clearly reciting
The myth of an outer world; its content: summer.

Who would have thought that blue could hurt so much?
This prospect also has forgotten time:
Along the shore the many-lacquered frieze
Of small waves lays a stationary touch;
The trees, as though self-mesmerized, all climb
Unmoved, you'd say, into a printed breeze

In which the yachts, remnants of an event,
Have long been left behind. Almost without
A cloud, the unimagined sky annuls
All qualms across the bay's embellishment
Which it exults above—except, far out,
A white dismay among the feeding gulls.

Diversionary Tactics

Surely, here at the heart of things,
Here is the ideal place for the attempt,
Here where the Christmas sales dispose
Their day-late offerings
(From which, it seems, scarcely a soul's exempt):
Whitegoods and videos,
The manchester, the saucepans and CDs,
The swimwear, lingerie that sings
The body and its moistening promises.

In parks and by the harbourside,
Along the crescent from the Opera House
To Lady... Mrs Macquarie's Chair,
They saunter, stroll and stride
In variegated thousands with the nous,
The timing and the flair
Of cast auditions for the late Buñuel
(Where the surreal is satisfied
In the plain day), determined to be well.

But on the train, leave them behind.
Among the suburbs summer has its way
And foreign scripts on once habitual
Shopfronts flash to remind
The joggling passenger that still today
Continues the old ritual
With a new but undeflectable endeavour,
For all that childhood has resigned
Its codes and haloed circumstance forever.

A few more stops and the wide blue bay
Waits with its yachts and dinghies and houseboats,
And around the shore big houses dream
In glass. Not far away
The beach calls in like promissory notes
Its combers, down which teem
With barefoot mastery boys who improvise
Diagonals across the play
Of wave and dazzle and their girlfriends' eyes,

But make no difference. And so
Just down these steps, along where that car turned,
The ranks of roses, the grass floor,
The notices that show
The times, even the names of those concerned:
James Whelan, Dulcie Moore,
Baby Joanna Harrington—and the eye,
Drawn by a low-pitched tremolo,
Watches the fine smudge rise in the summer sky.

Golden Coast

Adrift on the highest floor of this hotel,
I gaze beyond, around, between the boast
Of all the glassy towers which make their mark,
Their ulceration of the golden coast
Whose beauties they would sell,
Under the settling sediment of dark.

The miles of curving beach fade to the south
From where the lights as laggardly as sound
Struggle to make the passage of the gloom.
A plane's red beacon floats towards the ground.
You turn and kiss my mouth
And draw me from the evening to the room.

They say the end might come with little warning,
The climate breaking and the ecosystem
Collapsing almost overnight to pay us
The recompense of our belated wisdom,
Presenting in the morning
The advent and the only light of chaos.

Now, looking out with you held in my arms,
I see the buildings really are of glass,
Seen through and seen away with no more trace
Than last night's waves, the way cloudshadows pass,
The coastline's golden charms
Naked to view as you in my embrace,

Mapped and swept clear below us as my eyes
And hands explore your body's golden coast.
This day unknown to time will be there when
The light drifts through the shallows like a ghost
And dies of hours, the skies
And earth fall down and chaos comes again.

Nocturnal

It's midnight now and sounds like midnight then,
The words like distant stars that faintly grace
　　　The all-pervading dark of space,
　　　But not meant for the world of men.
　　　　　It's not what we forget
But what was never known we most regret
Discovery of. Checking one last cassette
Among my old unlabelled discards, few
Of which reward the playing, I find you.

Some years after her death, but years ago,
Hearing Gwen's voice recite "Suburban Sonnet",
　　　At first we could not focus on it,
　　　So jolted that the radio
　　　　　Should casually exhume
From our shared memory the woman whom
We knew and make her present in the room,
As though in flesh, surprised to find that she
Had earned this further immortality.

Who ever thought they would not hear the dead?
Who ever thought that they could quarantine
　　　Those who are not, who once had been?
　　　At that old station on North Head
　　　　　Inmates still tread the boards,
Or something does; equipment there records
The voices in the dormitories and wards,
Although it's years abandoned. Undeleted,
What happened is embedded and repeated,

Or so they say. And that would not faze you
Who always claimed events could not escape
      Their scenes, recorded as on tape
      In matter and played back anew
         To anyone attuned
To that stored energy, that psychic wound.
You said you heard the presence which oppugned
Your trespass on its lasting sole occasion
In your lost house. I scarcely need persuasion,

So simple is this case. Here in the dark
I listen, tensing in distress, to each
      Uncertain fragment of your speech,
      Each desolate, half-drunk remark
         You uttered unaware
That this cassette was running and would share
Far in the useless future your despair
With one who can do nothing but avow
You spoke from midnight, and it's midnight now.

Made to Measure

Impossible to wield
The acreage of the fabric that unfolded,
Slung from his shoulders like a crumpled field:
The distance from one Christmas to the next
When he was only seven
Was aching there; a foreign city flexed
Among the ripples; a face, the star-shocked heaven
About his flailing arms were shrugged and moulded.

Too heavy to outrun,
Too slow to measure what it underwent,
Though gradually the passage of the sun,
Unmanageable in its train of light,
Seemed almost to respond
As he yanked the yards of stuff in like a kite
And gathered the brocade that trailed beyond
His arms' reach to the scale of measurement,

However strange the weave
That writhed about the working of his hands:
The footage too atrocious to believe,
Printed with corpses; Greece; the falls of salmon;
Her upturned silken wrist
He would have torn out history to examine;
His father's final blessing, which he missed.
However far he comes or where he stands,

At last, and limb by limb,
Contour by contour, that unfolded cape
Settles ever more fittingly on him.
His forehead is the line of the sky's vault,
His shoulders trace the ground,
His palms the ways he wandered by default,
And in his gestures those he knew are found.
What shape the day discovers is his shape.

The Red Sea

Lulled in a nook of North West Bay,
The water swells against the sand,
Hardly more liquid than Venetian glass,
In which clear surface, just a little way
From shore, some four or five petite yachts pass
With languid ease, apparently unmanned,
Adrift along the day,

Imagining a breeze to fan
Their motion, though there's none. Siobhan
Reaches a giant hand down from the sky
And nudges with insouciant élan
The nearest hull, her bended waist mast-high.
That hand is just as magically withdrawn.
So moves the catamaran.

And through the Lilliputian fleet
She, Beatrice and Gabrielle
Wade in the shallows, knee-deep, spaceman-slow,
To fashion their manoeuvres and compete
Among the stationed hours to and fro,
While watching through the viscid slide and swell
Of water their white feet,

Made curiously whiter by
That cool light-bending element.
Doubled by shadows on the sand they glimpse
Pipefish and darting fingerlings they try
Impossibly to grab, translucent shrimps
Among the lace weed, seahorses intent
To flee the peopled sky.

Hard to conceive that they should be
Precisely who they are and here,
Lost in the idle luxury of play.
And hard to credit that the self-same sea
That joins them in their idleness today,
Careless of latitude and hemisphere,
Blind with ubiquity,

Churns elsewhere with a white uproar,
Or wipes the Slave Coast clean of trees,
Or sucks among the scum and floating drums
Of some forgotten outpost founded for
The advent of an age that never comes,
Or bobs the remnants of atrocities
Limply against the shore.

What luck they have. And what good sense
To leave the water with their toys
When called, before their fortunes are deranged.
And still the day hangs in its late suspense
For hours without them, virtually unchanged,
Until the bay's impregnable turquoise
Relaxes its defence

And sunset's dye begins to spread
In flood across it to the sand
They stood on, as though, hoping to disown
The blood of all the innocents he'd shed,
Macbeth incarnate or his grisly clone
Had stooped on some far shore to rinse his hand,
Making the green one red.

Memorial

(The lynching of Rubin Stacy, 19 July 1935)

In the still transfiguration of sunshine
That whites out almost all one leg and arm
Until they merge into the slender pine
He's hanging from with an inhuman calm,
Who are these blanched beholders gathered round
To contemplate the mystery they attend
With titillated awe?
What men and women and what children bound
In witness of the hour that they suspend
Lightlong? What shocked observance of what law?

Two little girls are standing at the right,
One staring at the lens perplexedly,
The other, half her face devoured by light
Bright as her smock, lifting her eyes to see.
There's one man whom the trunk obscures and slices
From view, a woman peering as though round
A door or window frame
At something not quite decent which entices
Attention even so, and will confound
Every objection modesty might name.

And then you see her. At the left she stands,
Behind the awful focus of suspense,
Her hands crossed, mimicking his handcuffed hands,
On her frocked crotch, her naked face intense
And lit up with a half-embarrassed leer,

A girl of twelve, maybe, too unaware
To mask her downward grin.
Sometimes the witnesses would souvenir
Some item: a photograph, a hank of hair,
A severed finger joint, a scrap of skin.

Surely she'll have no need of them. For here
This ritual and her rapture will unite,
Surely, into a lifelong souvenir.
This hour will hang between her and the light,
Between her and her life to come, this scene
And what she is in it will interpose
Imperishably through
The days that have to be the day that's been,
Lighting forever everything she knows
With what she saw, and knows she saw, and knew.

The Grand Hotel

for Les Murray

Apart from that, though, I recall
Something you said about the place:
That you could never see it all,
It seems to propagate with space;

Always another stair to climb,
Always another corridor
With other rooms to count like time,
The end of which is always more;

A sort of Tardis made immense
That somehow manages to flout
The laws of sense and common sense
By being larger in than out,

The three dimensions' mean constriction
Opened, unfolded and unpacked:
A building out of science fiction.
Or, come to think of it, science fact.

For don't they say if we could shatter
Their shackled forces we should find
Dimensions at the heart of matter,
Immensities wound up, that mind

Cannot conceive? That's some hotel,
And just the place to take to heart
And contemplate the parallel
World that this world is made by art,

Whose finite limits charge and prime
The senses they unpack, and store
Dimensions beyond space and time,
The end of which is always more.

Dreaming at the Speed of Light

Seen from that famous ray of light
Discharging from the town hall tower
On the last stroke of noon,
The hands would stand forever at that hour
As though the holocaust of blinding white
That set it all in train,
When present, past and future were triune,
Were come again,
The endless now on which the blessed take flight.

The falling autumn leaves would stall
Above the lawn, their futile red
A stationary fire;
The dog erupting from the pond would spread
In hanging glints its diamanté shawl
Of shaken spray midair;
The blue arc of the wave would climb no higher,
A gauze of glare
And water that would neither break nor sprawl.

And as that woman turned her head,
The streaming ripples of her hair
A painted banderole
Impastoed on the wind, she'd be aware
At once of all the living and the dead
And those whose lives would come
Embodied round her, bodying the whole
Continuum
Of all they had imagined and had said.

And every thought would undergo
This rallentando, every word
Would grind down to a halt
Midsyllable, interminably heard,
But charged with full intention even so
And purity of tone,
Free from distortion and for none to fault,
None to condone,
A knowledge only for the blessed to know.

Coogee

for Robert Gray

The sloping esplanade bends round the beach,
Flanked by a row of golden globes on poles
Which seem to leach
All other colours out of nine o'clock's
Submission to the ordinance of dark.
Against what must be rocks
At the blind limit of this yellow arc
What must be ocean rolls,

If it were visible. One orange beacon,
Blurred by some porous thickening of air,
Can only weaken
On Dolphins Point and slowly sink from view
As you draw near. Beside you as you pass
A solemn retinue
Of seagulls observes silence on the grass,
Under the dull gold glare,

Correctly marshalled and in uniform.
By way of contrast, milling on the sand,
A separate swarm
Of gulls obeys a separate motivation,
Shifting and standing, turn and turn about,
As in some installation,
Following steps the artist has laid out
And under his command.

The only figures still to claim the beach,
A couple and their capering child advance.
And when they reach
The avian artwork—pandemonium
As gulls peel back, fly up and reel apart,
Then gradually come
To rest, incorporating in their art
Disruption worked by chance.

As though to prove this *tour de force* no fluke,
The wind finds a black plastic sheet and flips
It up to spook
Their reassembled pattern. It spins past
And through their panicked order as they rise
And scream, raucous, aghast,
Above the yellowed sand into the sky's
Implacable eclipse.

The east looms heaven-high, black and horrific,
A cloud of nothingness that holds no trace
Of the Pacific,
A maw that tells the sheer end of the world
Columbus feared, in which those gulls are buoyed,
And some few whitely curled
Waves break, like forces bursting from the void,
Creating time and space.